DESIRING MACHINES

DESIRING MACHINES
ANDREA BRADY

BOILER HOUSE PRESS

OPEN SOURCE   3
HEADSPACE   5
THE DROP   6
STRONG DRESS   8
IN THE DAYROOM   10
THE LIZARD   12
WINNERS AND LOSERS   13
DESIRING MACHINES   15
HANDS ON FIRE   17
FERRET   19
31   20
CLEARING MY HEAD   23
TIP TOP   23
EXTORTIONATE   24
THE OXYGEN CATASTROPHE   26
DELUXE SHADE   27
A PINCH OF SALT   28
IT'S HALF PAST TWO   32
NONE THE WISER   33
AUTUMN SONG   34
HANGING IN THE AIR   36
ST LUCY'S DAY   39
KEEN   40
CATHERINE   42
'BURNED IN THIS ELEMENT TO THE BARE BONE'   43
SET IN STONE   45
CASTLE CARY   47
ALL OF YOU GONE   50
PIVOT   52
MERIDIAN   54
THE WINDOW   56
FUGITIVE   58
THE DETERMINATION OF LOVE   60

DESIRING MACHINES

OPEN SOURCE

There is an expression
there is not. The world is swollen with it
or I am, proper channels
are the ones that hesitate in the face
the mouth an anchor of that hesitation
which comes alive by softening
as a capillary does and breathes.
And what floods into offices and halls
where all the people are believing
they are not one

another is
forever there, the anchor or whatever dropped
into soft human tissue that is the bed
of the sea has no time
like the present to close
but this is its astonishment: that it can be
lifted and carried in a seasoned wood

channels an idea holding us
apart in fictions
of trade. The idea is not that life
we feel in our cells is ending
and drawing
a breath against these currents
is to exchange emptiness for poison.
Suddenly the rocks seem real and I can hear
how they too might be breathing,
the air falls around them regardless,
and water drinks them down.

I count on you
tapping hexameters on my insane
animal shell, dripping with differences
that have made history into a terrible fact I want
you to take the air
pressed from these sleeves no matter
who knows
any more what the mouth does,
if it cannot swallow
it might as well sing.

HEADSPACE

Through the tornado in the film a person
goes gritted and tearing, fragments of house
flying near but not through her head
her body not scythed but nearly
wind pushes her towards shelter
or her heroic aim. This is how her head
feels considering its detachment
from her body is too parched
to speak and quivering with need
for a dress, a strong dress
that would hold her, not plate
glass, not the devices
she worked so patiently in close-up
in rope and wire. These are images of a lost
country pulling itself out of the ground she thinks
only she can see, though others are also here,
also pushing, her face set
to the wind, her set of faces that steel
the present against every demolished town.

This is an instant, or a parenthesis.
Sometimes at sea, and everyone knows
the sea is churning. Sometimes cracked
in territories so dry they steal
blue right out of the sky. The person
presses forward, clear
liquids seep from her hands, her head.
No warning she can inhabit or slight
that fails to call her name, call her out
into the flat place, for she has people
she is saving
for later
cannot always be the same as now.

THE DROP

Waterfall I am, the kids say. The weight of
the person barrelling through me is not held
but passes and churns   under my skirt
where the flow stops. We look
back for a moment   as lights
flash and helicopters search for missing aliens
cryptic lights warning the city   I'm here for
ever   with adults   wading
through ghostnets
and the bruised child. She drops
like a raggedy doll   jackup rig legs
and semtex eyes   to the floor
under the thermostat   to the rug
braided from every archival colour.

I'm nowhere but standing   four feet on each bank
pressing flat a flattering image of the sovereign
fund with my perspex heel. That person is
someone different   wrapped in neoprene
ready to drop   completely over
the edge and wait   for a time to float.
But the edge is hard to arrive at,
people between here and it make a crowd.

One ankle clip is broken. I move
but not to help her   am pouring
my liquidity out for others until they ask me
to stop or drown them. I rush through my current
lovers   counting each
one held inside me differently   they sweep
me with their lashes and bristles. As they pass
over me I feel myself   turning into the drop
by which I know my fortune or even exist
is shallower than expected   and everything
stands in its way. Waterfall I am. Waterfall I am.

STRONG DRESS

When the time comes you are holding on
to a facsimile of hope: that beneath your feet
there is a landing, vulnerable fruit caught
in a net; that the interval between struggle and arrival
is just space, empty space, no complexities.

This is another way of talking
about being born. Falling into the world head first,
waking it with your cries, from the crate
of muscle and bone you pushed to its limit.
Arms around you contain what has no edges,
catch the parts floating away into material,
your parts striking other parts without meaning
harm. Drawn up into dark sleep
contained by bands dry wraps and secrecy,
you put on the human dress.

For a month strangers held
her hand, so great was her distress
seeks out an opening, is testing.
Another day it's a machine.
Belly full of engines and rotating blades.
You are strapped in, feigning confidence
and thrown through the air, out over the edge of the pier.
The hard surface of the sea conceals its endless
capacity to receive. Incessant the falling Mind
labours organising itself. But you put your trust

in engineers, feeling in the pit of your stomach
that this is a way of overcoming death, open to test
your fear of it; the interval
that separates you from solid ground
is just time, empty time, spinning on its axis.

Over your head goes the horse collar.
Your body strains against gravity and the buzz bar.
It's no longer clear who is doing this or where
the loops will give way to flat surface –
sky overhead, sea recreational
in the distance, your neck locked in its décor.
Hands release, ground is a muscle
throwing you away from the test of containment.
If you can survive one tiny duration you'll remember
what has always been true: ideas
won't be what finally kills you. The crane arm slows.
You get down, forget everything.

IN THE DAYROOM

On hot wet cloth. Above a square
stretched like canvas by street light.
In minutes, every one flicked, fidget spinning. Caught
between dream and its antidote: eating neither.
Watched, described, recorded. What am I doing?
My electronic bracelet prints my restlessness
on a screen: it spikes. I talk on the phone.
I'm smoking, in the corridor; in between
my manner changed and rambling.
I do not sleep but sing.
Demand exceeds need and you're laughing.

At times clean, at others filthy.
I cry for a sledgehammer, anaesthetic
to put me off my duties, a surgeon who'll commit
my hour to the bin. Split me open and take out
the militant thought roaming my cavities.
The cavities are dry. The thought
is big, swollen, and hits my reasons
with his guitar. Cut on strings, filled up
with nothing but verse, I roll
back, wrapped in dry sheets, certain this
is all being filmed.

If I surrender I might wake
availed of prosody, basically salvaged,
always fanciful, wound into understanding
the fetter of verse making my body
a clog while the mind goes free
wheeling into starry pastiche. But I don't

give in to care, and when the hard light arrives
announcing the assembly of other
people at their places
of work, walking to the bus, I'm already
in a new room, blank affixed to line end,
cloth and script changed under me.

THE LIZARD

One of my legs is bent and pink
a newborn appendage   not really stuck
to my hip   the other is long and dark
brittle   an elm stick   prosthetic candy
I test them swaying forward through windows
I levitate on paving and deliveries
It's almost impossible to give up the weight
to the woman I pay for emotional services

At rest I'm overcome with sadness
that flows from the socket where old and new bone
tangle with metal shavings   In my throat there is
a heavy reptile living he closes
the door I lean against listening for a passing voice
Will you hurt kids' club again?
What is your worst moment with children?
Would you like us to teach you elemental fighting?

   The reptile that was an egg
when I was on my feet in front of her
her eyes into bones   her metal in frenzy
is here now but only for me   When I release him
into the wild scratched from Camden to Philly
a wild of beings that flower and some that strangle
I can't know where he will disappear to
But he goes with a bang   a flash   of sudden yellow
leaving me behind with these inviolate children

Stretching their legs they leap out of stories
refuse to accept a joke for an answer

WINNERS AND LOSERS

So much is lost without first being
thought, a quantity equalled only by that
which is thought and never won.
You put your feet on the earth without any idea

and the earth will bear that, for a while. Infinite parks
full of infinite trees crowned by icy contrails
track human flesh escaping
form; they divide precise skies

into symmetrical parts that rest on your head
for a bit. A tune brings the chicken man here
the one who lived by the train tracks, covered in moss,
hissing at kids on our way to the water tower.

And when he burns down and the authorities
lose their grip on the machines making all that money,
the tide comes in under the boardwalk to threaten us
for thinking with our stupid inventions.

Nothing but kids who spent their savings
trying to make it to the beach are left. I got fried there
making kitsch and battery into drip castles, betting
on nothing but wages and my radiant indebted heart.

Half my head and body are in a zone
with all the things I didn't know to love
and have abandoned, the other with what I recognise
as calm that belonged to me only in passing.

An incision runs the length of my throat
and is tied with fishing wire to a strut of bone
that keeps my arms from hanging loose and ropey.
It leads me, or I lead it, scuffing

through mean dune grass, a sand
dollar in my pocket and my throat backing out
like the tide of money on which I nearly drowned,
a tide that looked like choices but was really

a line of foam marking
the highest we could hope to get
the limit beyond which
we needed no protection.

DESIRING MACHINES

1.

In one picture a mass is relieved only
by eyes, almond incisions in dark paint.
In another it is a mess of wire.
The body makes a composite apparatus that grins
teeth fencing off tractors, boxers
and hutches rumbling around inside.
This is the DIY melody, a message
sprayed on the wall of the way things are
built up by taxis and smoke. We go two blocks
north, two east, grinding down
the heels of our boots. We look
like an inscrutable mass. Feel like a tangle of wire.
On every stoop something greets us, calls to us,
and we reel it back in. Holes full of decisions and beer.
Surface tension prevents it all spilling out
onto the street, a riot of mechanical forms
scuttle away as soon as they are unlocked.
This tension is the body's to hold and forms
crystals on the brain. Somewhere it is also you:
imperfect, strained, plastic.

2.

Shop racks are lined with velvet, making me think
about prom, corsages and punk hairdos,
under the sea and being told
I would never find a man too unintimidated to love me
generous enough to listen to me speak. Even then
sitting under shaggy pink plaster
I recognised this as a speech about the past.

The future was magically individual
and though zombie fingers close
around my ankles every time I log out
I'm there, and not there, a holograph
flickering benevolently over that gross child,
flickering in and out of cold water flats
with you, and your kind.

3.

I reel in my desire, without reaching its ends,
without having found its limits are mine
and not mine. It sits in your composite face
opaque and mask-like and I look in your mouth
that promises bright Egyptian symbols
but it is never there. I can't test it.
I can just hold it, grubbily, my face pointing north,
my feet east. The sidewalk is rubbed
with scraps saved for work that could only be made
in bankrupt cities full of criminal fashions and bands.
I can't explain the danger I'm in.
I put myself there for this purpose, flight
backwards into grief that is neither
here nor there, the giant skull
in liberation colours now attended;
a trophy, bonus, type loose and emboldened
as I run around skinning these machines.

HANDS ON FIRE

It burns you with a clean alcohol flame
and this book is the channel of hot nerves
their steel-trap memories
along which fire looks for its exit.
You keep it hot in your chest
soft and sore behind your windpipe
you turn yourself upside down to shake it
into your brain which has recently cooled.
And looking at the body of your partner
whose shape seems familiar
but will always be remote and alien
you look for a sign there too, like the torch
that shows the fingertips are empty flesh,
but there is nothing, just the usual banging.

There is a fire on the street and on the common
set to showtunes and well-loved classics
there was a message that was received but not delivered.
Everyone explodes about it.
There was a suspension of fire in a book
about a boy who could hold time folded
shut like tissue paper, and everyone waited in case
something might be different on the basis
of a single decision. But nothing is ever decided.
You are waiting now, knowing you are too stupid
to underplay this guttering metaphor.

So you focus again on the fire in your bones
that makes you hold your front teeth in a perfect line.
Your skull is either grinning or baring. But now
you're gathering thoughts like herd animals
out in the open, where you can see them
and they are protected by the certainty

that only one will be picked off. You may be barking, or snarling,
but you are certainly waiting. History is not
finished with you. You bend down to take off
your need to be a container to yourself,
your slippers which are a hatred of genuflection,
you check the news and check again.
Empty fingertips strike a tempo on the nerve
that is the face still empty, the glass.
The burning outside is only ritual. Inside
you are consuming factories and houses,
places of worship, archives and emergency stores.
And the fire is less clean than it appears

it is also not dirty it's just a fire and your heart
is so hot now it could go up like kindling.
Would this be the end of your life, the extinction
of your compassion, or would your body
be flooded with the dumb magnificence
of a passion no one could ever imitate? You've no idea;
you shut your eyes and let it burst,
families coo over sparkling ordinance,
and finally someone says

the fire is here to burn
away not what you are, but all that you are not.

FERRET

The night comes forward wriggling its little tongue.
Everything that lives is dark against the male
wash and pink
phthaltes that soften city sky.
My desires are inky animals
that climb branches and pan out
through uncoiling streets. When I come
through uncoiling streets
my body unbuckles its silver girdle,
and no one knows the smell that warms
wet fur under the boiler, none but me.
Many names. The animals curl up in front of doors
and wander into rooms where they watch.
Green mirrors in their eyes give them
away to sleeping hosts. I lean forward
touching the fur coiled on your chest. Your mouth
a mystery to me, all the wishes lie
dormant inside it, I hook them and draw
them from their spools. It is this space between
what can be said and what can be touched
where I become the pulsing katechon,
limber with spices, hot as cast iron to the touch.
No I can't stay, can't stay. I convulse
thirteen times and lie in the dirt beside the fence,
little animals feeding on me in the dark.

31

I thrash around in my human body
when I sit across from you, shivering
like a split bell. The face I present
is a waterproof membrane, pinned at the corners
and tenting when the wind
gets under it, or someone does.
Other people could sit here and be still
but they are robots or dead.

Every restaurant in the country has a pair like this,
completely invisible to the naked
eye. At several removes
the possibility of your indifference
your business or even your dressed
body as it goes away should be a problem
of basic subtraction. But at this table, setting
a face as the wind blows it
into oblivion and catastrophic weather,
a face shaved with the effort
of being a person, beautiful, communicative, partially

composed: everything that could happen
hovers over it, warming fingers
left carelessly beside cutlery,
red indent on the belly where hooks press shut.
As it waits to be opened it buzzes with signal.
Under the cloth is a dangerous radiation
that can't be talked about but only shaped
with our standing bones, gathering
and packing it into an infinitely dense cube
to set in a sugar bowl. Someone will pick it
up and grind their teeth on it, shocked
by its terrible disappearing sweetness.

Let them. Those pins
propping up every millimeter of skin
leave a crawl space where filaments
run electrical fire, leaving the whole
building shaken and condemned. The ear drums
with a low bass, is licked out. The eyes
are tepid and milky. What is there to see?
Your chest is solid at room temperature. I feel it
shaking or is it me and does it mean I am
feverish or afraid, is that an announcement
of departure or arrival, lips
pressing insensitively on the cube of your heart?

In this climate nothing can grow on us.
Everything that has already happened starts
and the end is unspeakably close.
You might think I have been here before but I am
still green, still featureless, plucked
from the ground and ridiculous in the air.
The nerves in my back have been knocked off their pegs
to open ditches in the muscle
and let dry spirits float out.
It seems like me but I have no way of knowing
why or how not to burn
the pleasure of touch paper
is that its readiness is mine.

CLEARING MY HEAD

for an event I don't want to attend
that is happening inscrutably inside me,
coming to on a crowded platform:
a stranger bending over me, asking my name
an egg patched to the back of my skull.
For a minute I exist in the double space
that slices time from time, sound painfully
metallic on the tiled aorta of this blue whale.
Wanting to be neither blank nor dirty
I take a swig of air and cry into my music:
this is all your fault, commodified sentiment.

The hole is the false. My face is unrecognisable
to my computer in sun pixelated frost
but I'm in a hurry to get back to my project
mapping obscure spaces
no one can enter without being choked
by grip of data on my end
of life planning. The trees have held on as best
they can and make a gaudy show as cold
strips them, kids at school, coffee in my teeth.
I wake up, a little groggy. I peg out
the poem as a holding pen for all the wishes
I can't see, can't breathe
and put the kids back in it.
It is the watchtower they built from broken branches.
It is their violent animal energy
sticking their heads out of the canopy
stabbing their yellow brilliance into the sky.

TIP TOP

'Imagine you are a child of the grassland,
born out of an egg.' My son's answer
to my nervous loving that declares itself
in the assertion that he is perfect
just as he is out of fear
he won't believe me; a few words
that circle in the zoetrope indict me,
I cannot kiss better but make
a resolution to be perfect
day to day.

He asks me to imagine being motherless,
a wet form staggering out of a broken shell.
I am something that can be eaten.
But the grassland is there, wide and free.
How many other things does he need me to imagine?
Where will hunger take him, burn him
up when all he wants is to keep running
with the pack?

Milk
when he goes
pool at his feet.

EXTORTIONATE

There is a bird that mimics the car alarm

I nearly fall asleep at the table

My husband is covered in the ash
of work and I know his interests
only by the bumps and depressions

Somewhere my family is eating
turkey and debating uranium one and Benghazi
as salt water seeps through the pavement in Miami

Maybe these feelings can be classified as plants
Some are thorny, others covered in sap

Once I was full of rage that made me safe
The political was a mass on the other side
of the door of my lyric
Now I lie like a bolt on the spare
bed imagining how we will melt

The deputy town councillor said at the meeting
that our jobs are safe from the robots
until 2030 It seemed so precise
I could hardly stop to care about my fictions

The screw in my son's elbow is gradually working
itself free

Given permission to cross
I snapped at the squabbling and threatened
to go red and withhold their lullaby

The bird sits on my throat, the alarm is sounding
or is it the boiler too dear to fix

Comparing my psyche to Howl's Moving Castle
once the fire of the heart has gone
nearly out

Knowing that no matter how much I have lost
or saved
up against doom there is so much more
which could still drop off

this regal mechanism I have armed myself with
this faulty house and lumpen residents

THE OXYGEN CATASTROPHE

When the future calves for leisure craft
people making video applaud.
As it enters circulation it disappears.
That future implies there are people there
to keep time, but who can be
sure now, while riverbanks smoke. The hand holding
a shovel or camera shakes
with fatigue, hands have no time
for blessings, trees no time
to grow up to burn. Clay pots pivot emptily. Time
to go spreads like a warm blush
on the cheek of one who's properly latched.

We were told what to expect: gradual agreement, thrills
fading as the mechanic makes faces under the hood.
The gauge whose needle points to hot marks
the disappearing reasonableness of one past;
golden spike, profligate life forms,
all the animals still to be found in creeks and bogs.
Does anyone here remember how to live
without giving away what belongs to someone else,
giving away the secret of how I grew
my company into a multimillion-dollar business?
The future is a weak hand
squeezing a heart back into life, and warmer still
than flesh turning to chewy strips,
the slushies, skin polishes, dumb ticking of novelty clocks.

DELUXE SHADE

As if wearing a fancy collar of grief
in marching-band blue and gold
hair cut in secret code by the kamikiri
casting patterns on my neck and shoulders,
sky so interminable, answer so long
delayed by what could be
anything but ends in no.

For a moment birds sing again
about a coconut someone left for them
records of another climate that exists
alongside this one quartered in my body
stocked with perishables
and ineffective herbal remedies.

But then my fear flips around and I'm the guy who held a fish
up for a photo and accidentally swallowed it whole.
Its spines caught in his throat, but by careful leveraging
emergency technicians spared both their lives. Am I
the fish or man: the thing vengeful
against extraction, the thing
stupidly playing a part no one could anticipate?
What is written on the back of my neck?

Trees on sale, lights on.
Every morning the kids open another door.
Sweets make the loss
of light less dangerous, but shadows
are also voluptuary, gift of hot tears
drunk down as fortified spirit
into the well of myself. I'll suck on grief,
because to extract it would only leave me
full to the lungs
with spines and scales, gasping for home.

A PINCH OF SALT

Trial balloons mass by every shore,
    blocking the golden door,
    spiking the gold share and making the great
plains so far from equalising
bodies of water roll
their eyes over empty skies that they read at last
as free. To breathe free,
not the asphyxiating bubble
of the liberal traveller or water
boarder is not to be where blue jellyfish cluster,
    their deaths a distributed pain
    in the jaws of pets and seabirds
    who find them toxically free
    to eat and plentiful,
but to occupy the middle ground
in its extremity and stop its harvesting.

In an earlier disaster hikers turned back
uneasy at losing the sound of planes
that made their arduous journeys
    a miniscule, little blue nodes
    circling itchy pixels. Quiet
they knew something was
not right. Now the zone of exception
a few feet of arrivals, congress
    men with papers and men without
    driven back by a clown
who weaponises some archaic folk tune
and plays it and plays it to death.
You can bite, can scratch
everything you see out here
heads full of emptiness and fritters,

skies striped for shock in Yemen
    unlikely ever to be quiet.

Our enemies reply that nothing here is new, is news,
makes nothing happen, makes it new
post-factum and poems are lies; the bold
face already agrees, circling the pixels, driven
back now as in earlier disasters
by liberal guilt and container traffic,
the dead child out there is her brother's
image, I mourned him also.

    Now I've discovered
    an ability to make a great
division in what has happened my enemy,
I name it and its image, act distracted,
look at Beyoncé floating, steadily extruding
my view on whether he is sick or injured,
    demonic, possessed,
    a creature of chaos or of order,
because the DSM is easier to throw than Kapital and we like
to believe that we are seeing something we never saw before.
It is a way of valuing your life,
blanketed by work from shore to shore.

The stream gives pleasure, though no one
claims they're sleeping anymore, and poor Tom's
a-cold, he saw the future said fuck it.
Ed calls it being stuck in a washing machine
of misery. When we're close to weaning
ourselves history gives us its reasons
to return, circling the hole, filling and emptying it
    with detergent, hearts, data,
    till the comic overflowing suds of incompetence
    displace tragedy's curtains of blood.

I can't resist the urge to strap up
with my own bit of Americana, my passport
not compatible with illegal personhood.
    I have to confess
    I have never spoken freely
about my family. Their quote heroic individuals,
sentiments for the unborn and anger
whose pain can't find its container. The screen
door, broken porch, SUV
bumper sticker, Church collection
rented buildings after foreclosure
and weight gets put on
    month by month, like debt, concretion of time.
Fields of corn stretch up the hill, endless food
    that is not ours to be consumed,
        grass that is not ours but that we must
        mow forever,
and jealousy is unpatriotic as the red barn falls down
emblematically by the road. The blue sky

and the gold corn are legitimately beautiful,
even if they are painfully local. Once I tried asking them
if their lives might have been better
with socialised medicine, housing, education,
they said 'unicorns and fairies' but are quiet now,
    this future not quite what they intended
    but nothing they would fight to prohibit;
destroyed by capital, anger
and patriotism are the compensations for the lost
wish to stand up in the middle of disaster
        and live free
    of shame rolling out
the wage-earner's broken promises, laying his claim
on the shining city already under water.
    My father and I can't speak
about the quiet we make in the middle

of his hatred of my hatred of the country
that he loves, and loves the police, that makes
this hatred bearable. I don't know
if he has also been dreaming
     about being consumed by fire with his children,
or if that's my dream of our connection: to destroy

this future would be to destroy
either them or their pain, turning backs
against the plenty of which I'm a fiction
deporting the little that made these shores
like my chosen country's bluest sky unlivable.

IT'S HALF PAST TWO

and already dark; I'm shaking so much in the car
I seem to be having convulsions. The feathers in the air
are either snow or parting gifts

of birds who've had more than enough of my excuses.
For years I've watched this wave
gather strength in the bathyal zone

and now it is nearly here, I'm certain
the cutwater will never withstand it;
I look around at friends and relatives,

all of them too busy with clerical work
to scout for hills. Symbols crash, bullets point
and in the attic someone is fumbling with an axe.

I am looking for a bottle of milk to suck on,
for a giant balloon. The kids will be back soon
and the house creaks with preparatory heating.

Can I save them from the weight of water
that drops, they say, like little weapons
from such an outrageous height? It isn't

sunset yet, just a fragment of foreign thunder,
over the crumbled leaves and justifications
someone is piping crème anglaise

it is fear
it is present
the carols ring out its holy name

NONE THE WISER

I am warm enough to open up the world
folded into a practical square of brown paper.
My hand uncurls the fist in which a coin was hidden
but that's not the end of the magic trick
it's a form I wanted to use

this means to overcome
shabby backdrop, stricken events,
and through them the surgical scar
recently hot and trivial like a nail.
As if love was something other
than a cloth to wipe away ancient pain,
the common material each lives peculiarly.

I've put so much thought into you
that now it is returned it weighs me
down into the ground, I've put on an extra
16 kgs in my face is too heavy, it sags
over my shirt. When the tide
goes out it curls up on itself, makes a sound
of little coughing, in my throat a hive of bees.
This is how I know myself too full
of the body to share space with concepts.
I keep thinking

there is another way to make love
pliant and durable, to be immersed in pleasure
as hot and salty as a physio bath, or slop out
over the edges without staining the carpet.
But I can't try to find it by definition. None
gives herself away with her voice
trailing off her lip, her open code
open coat, because life is too short
it trails on the ground as she goes away.

AUTUMN SONG

Withdrawing from the blood bank,
my teeth a shower of sparks,
I cancel any unused promises
and scratch my cheeks in the dark

tottering state, leaves barely requiring
and gripped by a thread of cartilage
that becomes song. The moon is here too
as expected, hacking at the overlong heat

where the callicarpa bobs against a red
rowan tree. Songs tell an old story of long
desire, healed and frozen like a stick.
It is running out of places to play

in my body though I hold it up
with questions and pills. It won't continue
to rhyme, blood and moon, heat
and incomplete; my childbed

full of mice come in for winter.
A man stands on his balcony, gurning at death.
So many of us are disappearing these days
the weather is metaphysical, the wind

owes me a tuning an information
as I am arrested between old and young,
between men, between the wondering
and the answer

hidden in a snow bank, a snatch of fire
the thing that drops finally, losing its grip
the catch
the catch the catch

HANGING IN THE AIR

being less than an activity
we empty out the life that hangs
out there like code, but for how long
does it survive if the air is white and lush,
more benevolent than ever, leaves out
of a season everyone's missing. It hangs on
the front wall like a recrimination,
a rainbow trail, a wolf's chalky gasp
as he thirsts for the last kid hiding in the clock.
And like a call; and is filled with calls
of chattering species
whose voices are carried from house to house
party face time, many who last
breathe hard, hear them coughing like jays,
more every day going silent.

We like nothing more than indifference.
We pick our way prudently down the street.
Someone passing is like us
a matrix of infection. We turn around at the head
of the aisle that has another in it, pucker
mask wash and gel hands
and shrink. Hands very dry now. Mean
gestures all change, all change.

I say we meaning a family in London
who are lucky and have outside space.
The ball keeps getting kicked over the fence,
and there is someone there to return it.

A friend is repeatedly abused in the street.
Mean gestures, filthy speech. The street
where neighbours are clapping,

clapping clapping, instead of paying.
Where we perform distance for Lois
and Peggy's valedictory film, for the ages
less responsive, the random lungs
we don't know yet won't cope.
Try to contain the bad humours hiding
in another body. Hiding in a room that can't be left
the news, the violent partner, guard, border.
My psychiatrist brother-in-law says it's much easier
to get sectioned. We consider ourselves indefinitely
separated and weaponise incarceration metaphors and nothing
will be the same until it is, the amazonification
of the planet finally complete. We will party
like it's 1929 and write poems
upon poems about the virus and the discourse of war
still making no difference.

For now we pick apart the hem looking for silver linings
inside the garment of bad surprises.
We study black holes, clock time and dentistry in ancient Egypt.
I thought the singularity was a site of infinitely dense matter
but it's profound energy that distorts space and time.
The kids are overjoyed to learn that if they tried to pass
through its horizon they'd be spaghettified,
their whole body a stream of plasma
one atom wide. If your being was not then empty
it would be still, watching the universe shift
and quicken before it.

I'm standing up because I'm teaching
and working and feeding and remembering
and in pain and not remembering
what it was like not to be, the self that streamed
painlessly through another world not me, the light
stuttering on her face was not my light my face.
I was too stupid to notice how easy it has always been

to move down the street. I am reading
about the anaesthetists and misreading inhalation
of toxic gas as toxic glass. I don't want to think
of all the people alone

I tell the kids to write about their experiences
of this big historical singularity
and hide its data from them. I am stupid enough to say
the black hole can't be seen but shifts everything around it
but the kids know collapse
clears the air at least. How cool the sky would always be
without the scratching of motors. We could lag together,
smooth in our suspension.

We stay in the yard.

Its green and yellow is an image
of lungs we'll be given
if we cross the horizon and abandon
patriarchal family, private property, obedient domains.

ST LUCY'S DAY

Deep as the dark is driving
us it can go deeper, down into the rocks themselves.
But the rocks won't laugh at my friend
who is poorly for what he thinks
is his own fault, my friend whose husband
whose husband whose husband whose
mother whose partner whose teen son
is dead, flat, in a bag, my friend who has zero
for an original symptom. The rocks aren't worried
even by what we will scratch on them
with a cheap wooden stylus from Tiger.
As animals or accidents we may go in there
rooting around for an exit, following the smell
of diesel. We can't find our own way
out again without something to torch.
Ruined by love, lean and ordinary nothings
now in flesh appearing and now
tending toward stone.
The stars on the turntable vibrate
almost too slowly to be audible but they too
are making an extreme music.
Shivering in our immaculate furrow
lined with greaseproof paper and old towels
bones cold as iron when the freight train passes over,
the train that promised it would take our ancestors
somewhere, we hear what's really an imitation
but still belongs
to the immortal blackness of the year: drunk
till we are empty.

KEEN

Stars, put out your fires
for collection puts them back
into use. Here on the precipice
of a blasted year we scuff our boots
and owls laughing in the monastery
find it cute that we find them mystical.
A little knife of light sharpens the entrance.
It has done the same trick for a thousand years

but now it's doing it for us and we are doing
tax returns and pausing at the services
to think about an engagement
photo, a tulle dress, mulling a 1353
calorie burger. The car is heavy with presents
and the boy in the front clutches his paper bag
for sick asking the definition of nebula.
A cloud, but not like that one.

In my dream we were co-teaching a class on Voltaire
the child could barely stand, he kept pivoting forward
like a bird on a hinge, burying his head in fake snow.
This dream hides the dream
of women scratching their cheeks, pulling
their long hair out and cursing
men in metal outfits near them.
Their rights erased, they bury coffins
full of clay and exercise in the night
barking at trees until owls reply.
I've spent my life as a man

in armour, writing a statute
that calls me an organ of civilisation though my blade
is sharp enough. I've been a pillar of snow.
Now these women lift the lid and I'm starting
to understand their noises, as the long night of the year
closes on my griefs, my losses, the ones I own
and those I lament for credit.

CATHERINE

Feel into the heart, that perilous muscle
unknown, undaunted, when it shudders and scrapes
the world falls down on a distinct second;
but mostly it is proving there, undeterred
by sanction, passing on
information from the furthest reaches of the body
before anyone can interpret it.
Just between you and me
there is a plot of thistle, burdock, grasses
that last longer than the day I have to spend
in your company, imagining your heart inside me,
how we both depend on its continuation.
Some of you flicker out, some bleach or fade,
leftover grass gets light with abundance
of the unimperiled sun and rain flicks over
all the knowledge you had inside you,
your idea of old age, your small work
of inestimable value. You give out.
When you go back to where you were first
all I can do is devote myself again to the dream
of light that stays in materials, holding fast
all these staggering, unreliable pieces.

'BURNED IN THIS ELEMENT
TO THE BARE BONE'
　—WS Graham, from 'Seven Letters'

Younger in tenements and frothing
at the edge where the sea falls, you are walking
or climbing down or lying
in the dark where you turn
into a fossil or wreck. The tenement
is a holding turned property,
night lies on its outside until it is lit
and broken, what was austere
become a lavish candle of the living
worth approximately £5000 to the council.

> The eldest turn
> your face to the wall,
> finishing the air,
> growing up so high
> in a pigeonhole or warren
> all the children go out,
> Isaac Paulos not excepted.
> Fie, fie, fie for shame
> turn your face to the wall again.

Yes cry if you can, the night is hammered
by water that rises short
of where it is needed and falls back, alarmed,
sound of its falling and what is not
a screaming gull. Mark his
chin down, his puny gear not the limit
of his strength, he rushes out and back
like waves of heat but exorable,
in his humble ear the voice
asking why you left him. What's he to you?

Terrifying endurance of the body's
mechanics, and the limits of that engine.

May this pleasant month, now a helmet
of idiocy, standing for
nothing before the pleasures of June. This last
hot day, these bunches of flowers, sky
temporarily overhead. They could not move
on to a shelter beyond the falling leaves
of plastic, there is nothing for it,
their needless

deaths where these words merge and copy,
shameful filters still burning.

16 June 2017

SET IN STONE
for Denise Riley

The word lodged in the cervical spine
where it is smallest and closest to the skull
originally formed from spit and balled
up paper. A cruel word that refused
to look back at the boyish face looking
for recognition as water froze into a platter,
a congested mirror. And out here in wintry

dreamscapes of feathered ice, of men
capped and ballasted with sticks
for arms where feeling resonates without
chronology, all the words belong
to me: the fancy, the miserable, the hot.
I manage them all and pay
no taxes on the chance
that I might lift,
sheer air, out of my crinolines
through the cloud which is some snow,
which is over and above.

But there's a difference between being frozen
and being petrified. It's a matter
of one little name that ticks
barely perceptible in my neck;
against that crumbly dynamite, that deeper wound
down clock, all the other names I've given
myself are bragging rights
either of us left on the doorstep
of the graven house. In my sadness

a softness puffs. It changes limpet shadow
clinging to spurred bone to a limpid
shade blown over tufts. Blown off by just
such a voice as this: the voice who loves
these words, the homes you made in them. So hold

onto me, as words spill everywhere without diminishing
the quantity I contain; I am a spur, a song,
driven by repetition to say something entirely
new and listening to infants to learn myself. Take me
up. Uncover me, my hearing
creatures. Feel the funny lump
hardening in my throat as it melts, weather changes.
In that action of calling hope out
think that you are upon a rock; and now
throw me again.

CASTLE CARY

1.

I set off in winter – houses far up on banks, gulls
barrel-roll in heavy sky – and drive too fast
because the music is so loud, and my thoughts are full
of arms, heavy arms against formal sleeves,
I can feel them around me, exactly,
at what height, with what force, so many of them,
people now dispersed through short time,
some now on a train, in an office, stretched out
as if dead on a puckered sheet, around others
who also remember many like these.

I am thinking of the skin that edged them in,
stretched tight and thin over the rectangle
that held their life, my tongue in the dime
of their bellies, the black hairs on their nipples
and heavy warmth they carried in all spaces.
I can feel that skin against my cheek and chin,
and want to run over
the current to speak to them in whichever language
they speak now, that instant
is still inside me, inside this car and loud
song and everything I have ever loved
I love now and contain.

2.

Shapes getting less distinct, frazzled by water,
the road cuts in but the river sweeps away
it is hypnosis on the landscape
movement too slow to bear its history

makes a laughing-stock of me. In the hall
there is a replica of a mechanical arm,
and candles in the oven, rugs guarded by mist,
living narcissus threaded into shingle.
What is this feeling, I have to wash
my mouth out, with cries or songs,
my body is alone in time and when I close
my eyes standing in the road I am almost sleeping,
listening to sounds all over me.
The birds are individuals, citizens, agents,
they spread their many languages out
through the woolly, vascular sky,
one before me, others hovering behind,
each an instrument for measuring distance,
kinship, difference, they speak loudly
to their eternal appetites
and none startle or die.

3.

In the night we build a warehouse, everything
we need to live together is in it, a slide,
a pool, rotating cases for our shared media,
the next room is constantly surprising us.
Birds bring chunks of bread to the chimney pot,
then stand guard.

In the night I find the man whose appetites
sickened me. I am responsible for his post,
he quotes Shakespeare, is cloaked, he emerges
from his dark flat when a cyclist spills on the broken road.
The cyclist is repaired inside, the flat is full of party decorations
the man has grown so huge he can hardly be seen.
Or he has grown so light I can carry him
like a limp bundle of bedsheets when his meds

are ready. It is only when I lift him
that he recognises me, holds me back.
My mouth is what will bring him back
to health, I'm always working, as night
falls and birds take
the sharpness from clay pots.

4.

Now they have stopped. My book inside
my coat against the rain, my coat
making the only racket in forgotten night.
Surrounded by a comforting indifference,
vagueness refusing to pretend to speak,
all but a far owl who symbolises nothing,
scratching her living from the dark and staying put.
It reminds me of all my fears, hangers
of infancy angled in my dress, resting now
my body alone is not a target and this wood
not a way out. I told my kid about the witches
and trees that come up the hill like soldiers,
when you wake up it will be tomorrow,
but he still doesn't understand because this is never
what it is – the hills are the same, now is
always with him, like his fears of the future:
skeletons throwing balls at him, and his past:
the giant prawn ascending the stairs.

ALL OF YOU GONE

It's hard to think in sequence
when catastrophe comes through the airport,
or through a doorway guarded by police
who pick at magazines in latex gloves.
We were watching a film
about a man who turns into a cat and a cat
who turns into a man, when I saw them,
their fists pressed against their faces,
through the ornaments we hung yesterday,
as strangers carried him out. In my own arms
feeling what it is to carry them first
over the threshold, into the house,
rest there with them on the sofa
where they are born never to die,
waiting to become grown or nothing else.

I was cooking when I read the text
and later, in the bar far too busy, heard
that whether he deliberately fell he was
kept coldly for a week
by the police, and we would never know
what song came next though he jangles
in some galaxy on a blue chord
that has stopped progressing his dying
stupid and inevitable can't be spelled
if this country could be survived by anyone
it wasn't him, though I always thought
I could see him on a park bench, an old man reeling
and shouting prophecies at the sun. I was telling

her that he had been arrested when she said
he was dead, the thing in his brain had been
found when the thing in her brain killed her,
in October, in December, in May, their twins
doing ok considering, the lament from the west.
The thing in his eye. So ill, still working
for us on the handbook, her silversmithing
put down. And he too died, deliberately,
though I still know nothing
about the boy, lying flat zipped up in black.
It's too much to put down. Forgive me

for gathering your pieces together, broken hearts,
nothing works, whatever you had left
to do when you turned back at the edge
you could see at once the whole landscape
of what life you got, it was complete, nothing
called you back. And if the sun ever shines

as it did the day we bought snacks for later
when some go home for dinner and we would
be in hospital, bringing the baby out, calling that
a split in ghosts that glowed
brighter by the hour so we'll carry
on being dazzled by it even now,
zip, break, horn,
strange children stripping off to roll in clover,
fighting with sticks, wind and heavy goods
still in circulation, unashamed by any discipline
that shortens life we can't bear
to think is theirs or ours to cut down
fall on their face or slash with light
running metal into ornament while the phone rings
off the hook in an empty room for everyone
is outside on a day like this.

PIVOT

The light that pivots away from us
at your point in this year
makes you gorgeous and sleep
and always returns to you,
>   through the ellipse coloured
>   red for winter.

And the possibility of loss
is a sharpening edge whose peril
cuts your benefits
out in strong relief, it also returns,
>   not as habit
>   but as force that drives the work

that drives away death: this love of the earth,
this shining exuberance that needs
everything indifferently. The date
returns us to each other, across
>   gaps in sight and distances
>   that aren't so great, treats

the vibrations as motor blocks
tick over. Things are just diverse
kinds, everything in the sky
feeds them, nothing
>   is indifferent. We are two kinds
>   made in other images

but recently, and then our bodies slide
across pure mathematics
that rule their orbits, becoming less
    than one, a continuity
    can be trusted
    to keep

returning, whenever faded, through red
that casts our love in relief
a halo holding the whole system,
a field of work, a starry meadow,
    a human, you think
    you're the gift of all the gods you see around us.

MERIDIAN

A man coughing under the roof, pigeon squabbling
for sour cherries, I watch them go down its neck.
Slow cooling of traffic. Each day I fail
differently, having taken account
of the lines on the boy's palm that represent
a razor of light
as long and wide as the universe
and species death: an idea that is funny to both of us,
and leads him towards the idea of mine, promised to be
as delayed as the oldest woman in Japan.
Fierce fevers calcine the body of this world.
I shake and narrate it and fill with a sugary gum.

The artist traces the shape of his lungs in lipstick.
How else could we manage our limits?
By fantasising minds can be stripped
of decadent parts and uploaded to a hard drive,
to live forever in a hedonistic cycle that never tires
or gets curly like crickets playing
solemn nocturnes? I am always thinking
about you in a year's time,
your parts reassembled, records in different places,
the line break that gives song its form never
less than passionately enjambed but the new
body that is older and worse can't hook itself up here.

The door opens and what do I see. My hopes,
my sleepless imprudence, cloudburst intuitions living
still but moved a little further down the line.
And what do you see
of me underneath
this razor of light made of all the letters,
all the texts that cut through matter
in shadow where life continues.

Do you take me,
my excuses that little bit less persuasive,
my song sharpened on summer grass
and coming round and tailored in another country?
This is the secret
love makes me tell only to you,
and as the sun comes up and over we find
ourselves again in a different light.

THE WINDOW

Ricocheting off buildings and burned by the sun
that is damp in the daytime and dry at night
a great brush maligning the world that comes back
to it always hungry always deliberately poor

I go awry like an elevator confused by the shift
from vertical to horizontal I rub
off the face paint with a hand towel my limbs
are ruddy too the phone hot with limited use

There is a ghost here in the shape of a resident
something transparent around his shirt collar
I can hardly see the outline of his figure until
a wave of sorrow spills through him onto the floor

of a life that is a room bounded in glass
some cracked by bachelors some rippling with age
multiple plates annealed by anxious heat until
they can take colour, take human shapes

I can't explain how I have abandoned myself
in these rooms strafed by the sounds of mopeds
someone is pressing the buzzer too long
the insulation rattles so hard we are showered

with dust and fluorescent light with institutional
flowers and the crazy, brittle pleasure
that arrives by courier from nowhere and rings
around the sceptical day for entrance

The day was like that once now it is frank
gorgeous and penetrable the crashing city an open
field where people wander in small clothes
betraying their grace and getting numbers

I got lots of them and tucked them in
and fed myself and ate and fed again
muffling the sound of my hunger with my fist or not
at all and eating until I stretched across the floor

Singing a song I hadn't heard on the radio
for years but the words come back to me
a magic trick with parcelled energy I can't
explain to anyone from the past who knows me

They pull on the ear and fill it because it can't
be closed or sleep and so it waits
like this every day that is like this
for you to say what you were going to say

FUGITIVE

Light switches on planes start to blow
we are awake punching through the surface
with vowels. Each time I shift
to say what or where we are
on a swerving rock thrown forward
the sound is lifted by fires that roar
above this fragile basket. Skin gone pink
in the corner where the curtains
part you take
a breath from the air my body is heating
my body pressed like one of your sleeves
sighs and empties is also buttoned
and clean, fears softened by lotion
applied at your gentle pace.

For years before I came with my bag
and bones I was looking for you
and you were not there and then you maybe were
we both were now I hold the remnants
in each hand. Cool water up to your ankles.
Songs into your ribs. Now day is on us
an inch of merchandise and wrapped
panorama of a distant fabulous city
people we would never otherwise

see who is seeing you like the outline of a real object
fern of water, ceramic, through the tracing
and that orbiting vehicle mistaken for a fast star
my finger following bones that separate
your heart from the hard point of entry
threatening to flatten it. I asked you to take
the air you have
taken what you are breathing now, bring it
with you when you come
back to the landing place
fugitive refuge where you tick
like a hot engine,
like a wire or craft not wholly earthed.

THE DETERMINATION OF LOVE
(IN A YEAR OF FOUL PARLIAMENTS)

Having never learned how to fly or settle
into the dip where all ragged
voices go quiet, peace
curtained with patience, I write up
love's determinations in the middle
of catastrophes: a dramatic word for re-
cognition, the unforgetting of what
ever was never known, the cold open
where houseless identities appear at last
ghostly and luminous in the dawn
chorus a rage of twittering
no one can sleep in their own bed.

This story is covered every day
by the gift of tongues
and an understanding that feels
its way like a root pressing out
of the dark, towards luminous day,
though I say nothing
that's not already in the news
and can't help
turning the furious world's prolixity
into the proscenium
under which my luck plays,
plays.

My portrait of you is never equal
to your gentleness, and my tongue
that switches on when you open.
I recognise you by your shadow
at the door, your coming
home every day you speak
words I've never heard before
and yet I recognise them immediately
to be true. So it is dumb
how all my lines swerve around
your actual reflection, they avoid
containing it as they would forestall all
ends, the life
so short, the craft so long to learn.

(And you know I'm in the habit of not
refusing any way to be ungentle
about what a poem might have me

say.) About you I can say
something unequivocal – that you make love
a certainty, new crop
each year from old fields, new song
from familiar notes, you make
me feel like music
has finally been played
in a world I would never have other wise
made like this, not so noisy,
not so ghostly and catastrophic.

The case (full of rubies and seeds)
for sure we are
rests in a single voice
made of our two,
doubling and giving, sounding
then resting
for the air speaks too and with the phone
turned down is full of actual birds
each electing and singing roundels and debating
and recovering their makes.

The birds pick each other, and the fruit
from useless stones, hover
over glittering values they refuse
to recognise. The trees
they modernise are full of poisons
and the poem also breathes it in
to its small vesicles: but still sings, in smoke,
and judges, chooses, and you single

out what is nourishing
scatter a handful of stones in the field
of our belonging turn up
with juice on your fingers knowing
what each day is worth, what
will grow and with what you're saying
something certainly, so I learn
from you first
to jump out into the air
following your singular
voice with this
breaking
one into two

ACKNOWLEDGEMENTS

'Open Source', 'Headspace', 'Strong Dress', 'Winners and Losers', 'Desiring Machines', 'Hands on Fire' (as 'The Fire This Time'), 'Ferret', and '31' – published in *Critical Quarterly* 60.1 (May 2018). Thanks to Ben Lerner. 'Winners and Losers' takes its title from Bruce Springsteen's song 'Atlantic City'. '31' is a version of Sappho. 'Desiring Machines' was written in response to the Jean Michel Basquiat exhibition at the Barbican in 2017.

'Extortionate' – published in *Harper's* 336.2015 (April 2018): 16–17. Thanks to Ben for that too.

'Strong Dress' and 'In the Dayroom' were written for Beth Hopkins's exhibition 'Traces' at the Bethlem Gallery in 2017.

'Clearing My Head', 'St Lucy's Day', and 'Pivot' – published in *Poetry London*. Thanks to Ahren Warner.

'In The Day Room', 'Deluxe Shade', 'It's Half Past Two', 'Keen', 'None The Wiser' – published in *BathHouse* 18: Viscera. www.bhjournal.net. Thanks to Megan, Colin Wayman and Ann, and Rob Halpern.

'A Pinch of Salt' – published in *Granta* (14 June 2017): granta.com/a-pinch-of-salt/. Thanks to Rachael Allen.

'Hanging in the Air' – published in *Critical Inquiry* 47.2 (Winter 2021): www.journals.uchicago.edu/doi/10.1086/711431. Thanks to Hank Scotch and W. J. T. Mitchell.

'Catherine' is a memorial to the inextinguishable Catherine Silverstone.

'Burned in this element / to the bare bone' – published in *The Caught Habits of Language: An Entertainment for W.S. Graham for Him Having Reached One Hundred*, ed. Rachael Boast, Andy Ching and Nathan Hamilton (Norwich: Boiler House Press, 2018), 142–3. It was written the day after the Grenfell fire and includes quotes from Graham's poems.

'Set in Stone' – published in *The World Speaking Back to Denise Riley*, ed. Ágnes Lehóczky and Zoë Skoulding (Norwich: Boiler House Press, 2018), 143–4. It appropriates lines belonging to Denise (and to Shakespeare).

'Castle Cary' – published in the Organism for Poetry Research, special issue on 'Feminist Temporalities'. Thanks to Anna Moser and Ada Smailbegović. http://organismforpoeticresearch.org/

'The Determination of Love' – published on the British Academy blog, and written in relation to the Warton lecture by the same title, given there on 25 April 2017. www.britac.ac.uk/blog/determination-love-year-foul-parliaments-blog

All the poems above have been much changed.

Desiring Machines
By Andrea Brady

First published in this edition by Boiler House Press, 2021
Part of UEA Publishing Project
All rights reserved
© Andrea Brady, 2021

The right of Andrea Brady to be identified as the author of this
work has been asserted in accordance with the Copyright,
Design & Patents Act, 1988.

Design and typesetting by Emily Benton Book Design
emilybentonbookdesigner.co.uk

Typeset in Arnhem
Printed by Imprint Digital, UK
Distributed by NBN International

This book is sold subject to the condition that it shall not, by
way of trade or otherwise, be lent, resold, hired out, stored in a
retrieval system, or otherwise circulated without the publisher's
prior consent in any form of binding or cover other than that in
which it is published and without a similar condition including
this condition being imposed on the subsequent purchaser.

ISBN 978-1-913861-33-9